THE JOY OF LEARNING PYTHON

Rahul Saxena

I0011814

Published by Rahul Saxena

Copyright © 2021

All rights reserved. This book or any portion thereof

may not be reproduced or modified in any form, including photocopying, recording, or by any information storage and retrieval system,

without the express written permission of the publisher

except for the use of brief quotations in a book review.

Table Of Contents

5. Functions And Modules

- Introduction To Functions

- Syntax To Write A Function

- *args and **kwargs

- Lambda Function

- Map And Filter

- Variables Scope

- Modules

6. Object Oriented Programming

- Introduction To Object Oriented Programming

- Class And Object

- Our First Class

- Dunder Or Magic Methods

- Inheritance

Chapter 1: Basics Of Python

"Hello World", welcome to the joyful environment of python programming. I'm so glad that you picked up this book to gear up your knowledge in python programming. I hope this book can help you to enhance your knowledge in the field of Programming In Python.

History Of Python

Python is a widely used high-level programming language developed by Guido Van Rossum in the late of 1980s at Centrum Wiskunde & Informatica (CWI) in the Netherlands.

Python is an interpreted, high level language supports multiple programming paradigms like structured, object-oriented and functional programming.

Python helps programmers to write clear and logical codes and also allows programmers to express their logics in fewer lines of code.

Python is derived from ABC programming language, which is a general-purpose programming language that had been developed at Centrum Wiskunde & Informatica.

Rossum chose the name "Python" , since he was a big fan of Monty Python's Flying Circus.

Following are the highlighted events of Python history:

- **1991:** Van Rossum publishes first python version 0.9.0.

- **1994:** Python 1.0, Including functional programming.

- **2000:** Python 2 Introduces list comprehensions and garbage collection.

- **2008:** Python 3 fixes fundamental flaws and is not backwards compatible.

- **2020:** Python 2 is end of life, last version released.

Features Of Python

Python is a high level interpreted programming language that supports procedural oriented programming as well as object-oriented programming.

Important features of python programming are:

- **Easy To Learn** - Python is easy to learn because of its syntax free and developer-friendly language.

- **Freely Available** - Python is freely available, you can download it from this link https://www.python.org/downloads/.

- **Interpreted Language** - Python is an interpreted language because the code written in .py script is executed line by line.

- **Object Oriented Language** - Python is an Object-Oriented Programming Language because it supports object oriented paradigms like classes, objects, inheritance etc.

- **GUI Programming Support** - Python supports Graphical User Interface Programming. The most popular GUI module for creating the graphical application is **PyQt5**.

- **Large Standard Library** - Python has a large standard library which includes large set of modules and functions.

- **Cross Platform Language** - Python is a cross platform language which means it can run on multiple operating systems like Windows, macOS, Linux.

Installation And Setup Guide

Before writing our first program in Python, let's check whether Python is pre-installed in our system or not.

To check whether Python is pre-installed in **Windows** or not, go to cmd.exe and write:

C:\Users\Your Name>python —version

For macOS and Linux :

python —version

If python is pre-installed in your system then go and check the current version because the python installed in your system might be out-of-date.

Now let's consider those cases in which Python is not pre-installed in their systems.

To install python, either for windows or macOS, follow these steps:

- Download the latest version of python from - https://www.python.org/downloads/ for windows or macOS respectively.

- Now run the installer file and follow the steps to install Python.

- Once you finish the installation part, you can run python.

But if you don't want to write your code on IDLE(Integrated Development and Learning Environment) then there is one more option in which you don't need to download Python in your system.

So the easiest way to run python programs in your system is by using Anaconda Navigator.

To install Anaconda Navigator in your system whether it is windows or macOS, follow these steps:

- Install Anaconda Navigator : https://www.anaconda.com/products/individual .

- Run the installer to install Anaconda Navigator on your system.

- Open Anaconda Navigator and launch Jupyter Notebook(**Jupyter Notebook** is an open-source web application that allows you to create and share documents that contain live code, equations, visualisations and narrative text).

- Create a new file and start writing your programs.

First Program In Python

In our previous section, we successfully downloaded python in our system. So now this is the right time to write our first python program.

Let's write our first program on IDLE,

You can only write your code in IDLE only if you successfully downloaded and installed python in your system.

- Type python in the command line(Windows) or terminal(macOS), invokes the interpreter.

- Type 1+1 and this will give you an output 2.

- To exit this mode, type quit() and press enter.

If you want to display "Hello World" in IDLE, we use command :

>>>print('Hello World')

O/p - Hello World

In above statement print command display the message Hello World.

This is the case when you installed python and want to use IDLE but what if you want to use IDE's. In that case just open your IDE, if using text editors like sublime text editor in that case save your python program with .py extension and run it using command line or terminal else if you're using proper software or environment like Pycharm or Spyder IDE then just write your code and run it.This will give you proper output.

Comments

Comments play a crucial role while writing our source code because it's necessary to make your code easy to understand by others.

With the help of comments, we can make our source code more readable.

Like in another programming languages, python also having two types of comments:

1. Single Line Comment

2. Multi-Line Comment

To add a single line comment in python, we use the hash symbol #. The statement written after # will be completely ignored by python interpreter.

For Example :

    # This is a single line comment.

    # Hello World

To add a multi-line comment in your code either you can add hash # symbol for each line.

    # Hello This

    # Is A

    # Multiline Comment.

Or else you can use multiline string. Since Python ignores string literals that are not assigned to a variable, you can add a multiline string (triple quotes) in your code, and place your comment inside it.

For Example:

```
"""

Hello There

This Is A Multi-line Comment

"""
```

Variables

Suppose that you want to store values or data in your computer memory but what if you want to reuse stored data ? How can you retrieve your data from memory ? Answer is you need the location of memory(address) where you stored your data.

If you want to reuse your data in that case you can use Variables.

Variables are like box or containers which stores your data.

Python has no command to declare a variable. Variable is created the moment we assign value to a variable.

For Example :

```
var_name=value
```

In Python variables are dynamically typed which means you can change value of your variable anytime.

For Example:

x=5

x=12.5

In the above example, first I stored 5 inside my variable(which is an integer type) but after that I reassigned value to my variable x(which is a decimal type).

So above example properly states that Variables in Python are Dynamically Typed.

Rules for choosing right variable name:

- A variable name must start with a letter(either lowercase or uppercase) or the special character underscore(_).

- A variable name cannot start with a number.

- You can't use characters like @,#,$ etc in your variable name.

- A variable name only consists of alphanumeric characters and underscore.

For Example :

1. **Valid Variable -** _var , var2 etc.

2. **Invalid Variable -** var@ , var var etc

Variables are case sensitive in python which implies that,

_var is not same as _Var.

Operators

Operators are used to perform basic Arithmetic or Logical operations on variables or values.

The value that the operator operates on is called the operands.

For Example:

2+3=5

where 2,3 are operands and + is an operator.

In Python we have 7 types of operators:

1. Arithmetic Operators

2. Compound Assignment Operators

3. Comparison Operators

4. Logical Operators

5. Identity Operators

6. Membership Operators

7. Bitwise Operators

Let's have a brief explanation of all the operators one by one.

Arithmetic Operator : Arithmetic Operators are used to perform basic mathematical operations on the operands.

Operator	Operator Name	Example	Output
+	Addition	2+1	3
-	Subtraction	2-1	1
*	Multiplication	2*1	2
/	Division	2/1	2.0
%	Modulus	2%1	0
**	Exponentiation	2**1	2
//	Floor Division	5//2	2

Note : In Python, division of two integer values returns a decimal type value.

Floor Division - Floor Division is similar to normal division but it removes decimal part of the output(without rounding up the value).

Comparison Operators: Comparison Operators are used to perform comparison between two operands.

Operator	Naming	Example
>	Greater Than	x>y
<	Less Than	x<y
!=	Not Equal To	x!=y
>=	Greater Than Or Equal To	x>=y
<=	Less Than Or Equal To	x<=y

Note :

- Greater Than Operator returns true if left side operand is greater than right side operand.

- Less Than Operator returns true if left side operand is less than right side operand.

- Equal To(==) Operator returns true when both the operands are equal.

- Not Equal To Operator returns true when both the operands are not equal.

- Greater Than Or Equal To Operator returns true when left operands is greater than or equal to the right operand.

- Less Than Or Equal To Operator returns true when left side operands is less than or equal to the right side operand.

Logical Operator : Logical Operator is used to perform logical operations between two operands.

Operator	Example
and	x<2 and x<5
or	x<3 or x>1
not	not(x<3 or x>1)

Note :

- and Operator returns true if both the expressions return True.

- or Operator returns true if one of the expression return True.

- not Operator Reverts the results means if true then false and if false then true.

Compound Assignment Operator: Compound Assignment Operators are used to assign value to the variable.

=	x = 5	x = 5
+=	x += 3	x = x + 3
-=	x -= 3	x = x - 3
*=	x *= 3	x = x * 3
/=	x /= 3	x = x / 3
%=	x %= 3	x = x % 3
//=	x //= 3	x = x // 3
**=	x **= 3	x = x ** 3
&=	x &= 3	x = x & 3
|=	x |= 3	x = x | 3
^=	x ^= 3	x = x ^ 3
>>=	x >>= 3	x = x >> 3

Identity Operator : Identity operators are used to check if they are actually the same object, with the same memory location or not.

Operator	Example
is	x is y
is not	x is not y

Note :

- is Operator returns true if both the objects are same.

- is not Operator returns true if both the objects are not same.

Membership Operator : Membership Operator is used to check if the value or a sequence is present in the given object or not.

Operator	Example
in	x in y
not in	x not in y

Note :

- in operator returns true if a value or a sequence is present in a given object.

- not in operator returns true if a value or a sequence is not present in a given object.

Bitwise Operator : Bitwise Operators are used to compare binary numbers.

- AND(&) - Sets each bit to 1 if both bits are 1.

- OR(|) - Sets each bit to 1 if one of two bits are 1.

- XOR(^) - Sets each bit to 1 if only one of two bits are 1.

- NOT(-) - Inverts all the bits.

- Left Shift(<<) - Shift left by pushing zeroes in from the right and let the leftmost bits fall off.

- Right Shift(>>) - Shift right by pushing copies of the leftmost bit in from the left, and let the rightmost bits fall off.

Chapter 2: Data types In Python

In the previous chapter, we learned about how to assign value to our variable and also learned how to perform arithmetical or logical operations on that value but what if we say that the values we assigned to our variables are of different types ?

Answer is Yes, we have different types of values to assign to our variables and this is what we called Data Type.

Datatype is a type of data that we assign to our variables.

In Python, datatypes are classified into two types,

1. Primitive Datatype

2. Non-Primitive Datatype

Primitive Data types : Data types that are pre-defined and supported by the programming language are called primitive data types.

For Example : Integer , float , string , boolean.

Non-Primitive Data types : Data types that are derived from primitive data types are called non-primitive data types.

For Example : List, tuple, dictionary, sets.

Let's have a brief knowledge of datatypes of python.

Integers

Integers are the numbers that can be positive, negative, or zero, without decimals.

For Example : -4, -2,0, 3, 55 etc

Floating Point

Floating Point are the numbers that can be positive, negative, with decimals.

For Example : -4.0, 3.22, 55.3 etc

Strings

Strings are a sequence collection of characters written inside either single quotes or double-quotes.

For Example: "Hello World" , 'String Here'.

Note :

- Strings are immutable, means we cannot modify our string literals once assigned.
- Strings allows concatenation, which means we can add any number of strings and this will result us a new string.
- Strings are ordered sequence of characters which means indexing and slicing are allowed.

Indexing : Indexing allows us to grab single character from string.

Syntax to grab a single character,

String[index_of_character]

Python strings are 0-indexed. So the first character is 0, second is 1, so on. So if the there are n characters in a string, the last character is n-1.

You can access the elements at the end by adding a minus.

Indexing of characters in a string can be positive and negative.

For Example:
"STRING"[1]="T"
"STRING"[-1]="G"
"STRING"[-4]="R"
"STRING"[4]="N"

Slicing : Slicing allows us to grab a subsection of multiple characters from string.

Syntax Of Slicing Is,

String[start:stop:step]

start: start is a starting index.
stop: stop is an ending index(where slicing stops).
step: step is an index used to specify the steps from starting index to ending index.

All these parameters are optional – the default value of start is 0, the default value of end is the length of string and the default value of step is 1.

For Example :

"STRING"[:]="STRING"
"STRING"[:2]="ST"
"STRING"[1:3]="TR"
"STRING"[::2]="SRN"
"STRING"[:-2]="STRI"
"STRING"[-4:-2]="RI"
"STRING"[::-1]="GNIRTS"   # Returns Reverse

Concatenation : String concatenation means addition of multiple strings together.

For Example :

"This Is My"+" String" = "This Is My String"
"Hello"+"World"="HelloWorld"

Methods Of String

Methods are the functions belongs to an object.

Let's discuss few important methods of strings,

1. **capitalize()**: Converts the first character to uppercase.
2. **count()**: Returns the number of times a specified value occurs in a string.
3. **find()**: Search the string for a specified value and returns the position of where it is found.
4. **lower()**: Coverts a string into lower case.
5. **upper()**: Converts a string into upper case.
6. **split()**: Splits the given string at the specified separator and returns a list.

So these are few basic methods of string.

String Formatting

String formatting lets you inject items into a string.

A string includes three types of formatting:

1. Using % character
2. Using .format()
3. Using f-strings

Case 1: Using %s character,

You can use %s to inject strings into your print statements. The modulo % is referred to as a "string formatting operator".

For Example :

```
print("Hello %s How Are You"%'World')
```

```
O/p - Hello World How Are You
```

We can also pass multiple variables,

x="World"
y="Are"
```
print("Hello %s How %s You"%(x, y))
```

```
O/p - Hello World How Are You
```
Floating point numbers use the format %3.2f. Here, 3 would be the minimum number of characters the string should contain; these may be padded with whitespace if the entire number does not have this many digits. Next to this, .2f stands for how many numbers to show past the decimal point. Let's see an example:

```
print('Floating point numbers: %5.2f' %(13.144))
```

O/p - Floating point numbers: 13.14.

Case 2 : Using .format()

.format() introduced as advanced version of string formatting.

For Example :

print("Hello {} How Are You".format("Ryan"))

O/p - Hello Ryan How Are You

For insertion of multiple strings,

print("Hello {} How {} You".format("Ryan","Are"))

O/p - Hello Ryan How Are You

Also We Can Use Index Positions To Inject Values,

print("Hello {0} How {1} You".format("Ryan","Are"))

O/p - Hello Ryan How Are You

print("Hello {1} How {0} You".format("Ryan","Are"))

O/p - Hello Are How Ryan You # wrong sentence but consider it # just an example.

For Float Precision,

Syntax - {value:width.precision}

num=23.45678

print("four decimal number is:{0:10.4f}".format(num))

O/p - four decimal number is 23.4568

Case 3: Using f-string

f-string formatting is similar to .format() formatting but, f-string formatting introduced as latest version of string formatting with advanced features.

For Example :

x="Ryan"

print(f'Hello {x}')

O/p- Hello Ryan

For Multiple Insertion,

x="Ryan"
y="Daniel"

print(f'Hello {x} {y}')

O/p- Hello Ryan Daniel

For Float Precision,

Syntax Is - {value:{width}.{precision}}

For Example -

num=23.45

print(f"four decimal number is:{num:10.4f}")

O/p - four decimal number is   23.4500

List

List are collection of order sequence of various object types in python.

List holds various object types inside square brackets separated by comma(,).

For Example :   x=[object_type_1, object_type_2].

Object Types : Integers, floating point , strings , set , tuples , dictionary , and even list itself.

Note :

- Lists are mutable, which means we can modify(add and delete objects) our list according to our need.

- Lists are order sequence of various object types, means Indexing and slicing are allowed.

- A list allows concatenation, **which** means we can add multiple lists.

Indexing: Indexing allows to grab single object type from list.

Syntax To Grab A Single Object Type Is,

list_name[index_of_object_type]

Indexing of a list is similar to indexing of a string but in a list, we are picking up an object type and in a string, we picked up a character.

List also allows positive and negative indexes likewise in strings.

For Example :

```
x=[1, 2.5, "Hello"]
x[0]=1
x[-1]="Hello"
```

Slicing : Slicing allows to grab a subsection of objects from list.

Syntax Of Slicing Is,

```
list_name[start:stop:step]
```

For Example :

```
x=[1, 2.5, "Hello", 3, "World"]
x[:]=[1, 2.5, "Hello", 3, "World"]
x[1:]=[2.5, "Hello", 3, "World"]
x[2:4]=["Hello", 3]
x[2:-1]=["Hello", 3]
x[::2]=[1, "Hello", "World"]
```

Note : x[::-1] returns reverse of a list.

Concatenation : List concatenation means addition of multiple lists together.

For Example :

```
x=[1,2,3]
y=[4,5]
x+y=[1,2,3,4,5]
```

Methods Of List

Methods are the functions belongs to an object.

Let's discuss few basic methods of list,

- **append()**: Adds an element at the end of the list.
- **clear()**: Removes all the elements from the list.
- **copy()**: Returns a copy of the list.
- **extend()**: Add the elements of a list(or any iterable), to the end of the current list.
- **index()**: Returns the index of the first element with the specified value.
- **insert()**: Add an element at the specified position.
- **pop()**: Removes the element at the specified position.
- **remove()**: Removes the first item with the specified value.
- **reverse()**: Reverses the order of the list.
- **sort()**: Sorts the list.

Tuples

Tuples are collection of order sequence of different object types like a list, but the difference is tuples are immutable.

Tuples holds different object types inside parenthesis separated by comma.

For Example : x=(1, "Hello", 2.5)

Note :

- Python tuples have a surprising trait: they are immutable, but their values may change. This may happen when a tuple holds a reference to any mutable object, such as a list.

- Tuples are order sequence of various object types, which means Indexing and slicing are allowed.

- Tuple allows concatenation, **which** means we can add multiple tuples.

Indexing, slicing, and concatenation of a tuple is similar to the indexing, slicing, and concatenation of a list.

So, let's jump to methods of Tuples,

1. **count():** Returns count of a specified value in a tuple.

   For Example -

   ```
   x=(1,2,1,2,1,2,1)
   print(x.count(1))
   O/p = 4
   ```

   Because 1 occurred 4 times in our tuple.

2. **index():** Returns the first index of the specified element in the tuple.

   For Example -

   ```
   x=(1,2,1,2,1,2,1)
   print(x.index(2))
   ```

$$O/p = 1$$

Because index of first 2 is 1.

Dictionary

Dictionary is an unordered mapping of objects in the form of key-value pairs.

Dictionary holds objects in the form of key-value pair inside curly braces and each key-value pair is separated by comma.

In a dictionary, two same keys are not allowed either for the same value or for the different values.

For Example :

$$x=\{'Name': "Ryan", 'Age': '22'\}$$

So, if you want to access value of a key then you should mention key of that specified value.

For Example :

```
x={'Name': "Ryan", 'Age': '22'}
print(x['Name'])
O/p- "Ryan"
```

Dictionary are unordered mappings of key-value pair, that's why we cannot apply **Indexing and slicing** on dictionary.

Note:

- In a dictionary, keys are immutable but value associated to that key is mutable.

To change the value of a specified key,

    dictionary_name[key_name]=new_value

For Example:

    x={'Name': "Ryan", 'Age': '22'}
    print(x['Name'])
    O/p- "Ryan"
    x['Name']="Rahul"
    print(x['Name'])
    O/p- "Rahul"

Methods Of Dictionary :

clear(): This method is use to remove all the key-value pairs from a dictionary.

For Example:

    x={'Name': "Ryan", 'Age': '22'}
    x.clear()
    print(x)
    O/p-{}

get(): This method is use to find value of a specified key.

For Example:

```
x={'Name': "Ryan", 'Age': '22'}
print(x.get("Name", "Not Found")
O/p-"Ryan"
```

In the above example if a key is present in the list then the method will return a value associated with that key otherwise returns the message you will mention, like I mentioned: "Not Found".

items ( ): This method is use to return a list containing tuples of each key-value pair.

For Example:

```
x={'Name': "Ryan", 'Age': '22'}
print(x.items())
O/p- [('Name', "Ryan"), ('Age', '22')]
```

keys ( ): This method is use to return a list of all keys in a dictionary.

For Example:

```
x={'Name': "Ryan", 'Age': '22'}
print(x.keys())
O/p-['Name', 'Age']
```

values ( ): This method is use to return a list of all values in a dictionary.

For Example:

```
x={'Name': "Ryan", 'Age': '22'}
print(x.values())
O/p-["Ryan", '22']
```

pop(): This method is used for removing key-value associated with that specified key.

For Example:

```
x={'Name': "Ryan", 'Age': '22'}
x.pop('Name')
print(x)
O/p-{'Age': '22'}
```

So these are few important methods of a dictionary.

Sets

Sets are unordered sequence of unique elements.

Sets holds unique values of different datatypes inside curly brackets.

For Example :

```
my_set={1, "a" ,2.5}
print(my_set)
O/p-{1, "a" ,2.5}
```

Note:

- Sets are unordered collection of unique objects.
- Sets are unchangeable means we cannot change items once assigned.

The only way to access elements of sets is looping.

For Example:

```
my_set={1, "a" ,2.5}
for I in my_set:
        print(I)
O/p- 1
        'a'
        2.5
```

Methods Of Sets:

add (): This method is used for adding elements to your sets.
For Example:

```
my_set={1, "a" ,2.5}
my_set.add(4)
print(my_set)
O/p- {1, 'a', 2.5, 4}
```

clear (): This method is use to remove all the objects from set.

For Example:

```
my_set={1, "a" ,2.5}
my_set.clear()
print(my_set)
O/p- set()
```

discard(): This method is use to remove specified element from set.

For Example:

```
my_set={1, "a" ,2.5}
my_set.discard('a')
print(my_set)
O/p- {1, 2.5}
```

Type Casting In Python

Type Casting is the method to convert the object or variable datatype into certain datatype.

In Python, we have two types of casting:

1. **Implicit Casting:** Converts a datatype into another datatype internally(without use of any function).

For Example: Division of two integers in python automatically result a floating point value.

```
x=2
y=10
print(y/x)
O/p=5.0
```

2. Explicit Casting: Converts a datatype into another datatype using pre-defined functions like int(), float(), str().

For Example:

- Integer to Floating Point.
- Integer to String.
- Floating Point to Integer.
- Floating Point to String.
- String To Integer.
- String To Floating Point.

So Let's discuss all these type castings one by one.

Integer to Floating Point: To convert an integer type to a floating-point, we use the float() function.

For Example:
```
x=3
x=float(x)
print(x)
O/p-3.0
```

Integer to String: To convert an integer type to a string, we use the str() function.

For Example:
```
x=3
x=str(x)
print(x)
O/p-"3"
```

Floating Point to Integer : To convert a floating-point to an integer type, we use the int() function.

For Example:

```
x=3.8
x=int(x)
print(x)
O/p-3
```

Integer conversion removes decimal point without rounding up the value.

Floating Point to String: To convert a floating-point to a string, we use the str() function.

For Example:

```
x=3.2
x=str(x)
print(x)
O/p-"3.2"
```

String to Integer: To convert a string to an integer type, we use the int() function.

For Example:

```
x="3"
x=int(x)
print(x)
O/p- 3
```

This will give error if we try to convert decimal containing string or alphabets to an integer.

String to Floating Point: To convert a string to floating point, we use the float() function.

For Example:

x="3.2"
x=float(x)
print(x)
O/p-3.2

This will give an error if we try to convert non numeric characters to the floating point.

Chapter 3: Conditional Statements

Conditional Statements are decision making statements in python.

In Python we have four types of conditional statements:

1. if statement

2. if-else statement

3. if-elif-else statement

4. Nested if statement

Let's discuss all four conditional statements one by one.

if statement

Whenever we have a single condition to check, In that case we use if statement.

Statements inside if block executes if and only if the expression followed by if statement returns true.

Syntax of if Statement:

```
if expression(s):
    #statement
    #statement
```

The above syntax consists of if keyword followed by an expression(s), and the statements.

Flowchart of if statement states that if the condition followed by the if statement returns True then only the body of the if statement will execute otherwise interpreter will jump to the next statement.

For Example:

Let's write a program to check whether a given number is positive or not.

```
x=3
if x>0:
        print("Positive Number")
```

O/P- Positive Number

if-else statement

An else statement contains the block of code that executes if the expression in the if statement returns FALSE.

Syntax of if-else Statement:

```
if expression:
        #statements
        #statements
else:
        #statements
        #statements
```

Syntax of if-else statement consists of if block(followed by an expression)and the else block.

Note: else statement do not have any condition to check and executes only if, expression followed by if statement returns false.

Flowchart of if-else statement states that if the condition followed by the if statement returns True then only the body of the if statement will execute otherwise body of the else statement will execute.

For Example:

Let's check whether a given value is positive or negative.

```
x=3
if x>0:
        print("Positive Number")
else:
        print("Negative Number")
```

O/P- Positive Number

if-elif-else statement

Whenever we have multiple conditions to check(where different conditions results different output) in that case we use if-elif-else statement.

elif statement allows us to check multiple expressions and executes a block of code as soon as one of the conditions evaluates True.

There can be multiple 'elif' blocks.

Syntax of if-elif-else Statement:

```
if  expression:
        #statements
        #statements
elif expression:
        #statements
        #statements
elif expression:
```

```
        #statements
        #statements
else:
        #statements
        #statements
```

Flowchart of if-elif-else states that if the condition followed by if statement return false then interpreter will check condition followed by upcoming elif statements and if all the conditions return false in that case interpreter will execute the block of statements followed by else block.

For Example :
Let's check greatest among 3 integers.

```
x=2
y=3
z=4
if x>y and x>z:
    print("x is greatest")
elif y>x and y>z:
    print("y is greatest")
else:
    print("z is greatest")
```
O/P- z is greatest

Nested if Statement

If we have chain of conditions to check, then we called it a Nested if statement.

Nested if statement is like conditions followed by another conditions.

Syntax Of Nested If Statement:

```
if expression:
    if expression:
        #statements
        #statements
    else:
        #statements
        #statements
else:
    #statements
    #statements
```

Above Syntax states that we can have any number of if statements inside any conditional statements.

For Example :

In this example, we will check whether given number is positive or negative or zero.

```
x=int(input("Enter Your Number"))
if x>=0:
    if x==0:
        print("Zero")
    else:
        print("Positive")
else:
    print("Negative")
```

In the above example, if we assign integer value greater than equal to zero to x than this will recheck condition for Zero, if false then output Positive Number and if number is less than zero then output will be "Negative" number.

Chapter 4: Looping Statements

In our everyday life we repeat multiple tasks, sometimes for short duration of time and sometimes for long duration. This repetition of tasks is called looping.

Similarly, looping statements in python states that if condition is true **then** sequence of statements will executes for multiple times.

For Example :

You put your favorite song on a repeat mode. It is also a loop.

In Python, we have three types of looping statements,

1. for loop

2. while loop

3. Nested loop

Let's discuss all the looping statements one by one.

for loop

for loop is a looping statement in python, used for iterating over a sequence.

For Example:

Suppose that our task is to print all the numbers from zero to hundred. In this case, we prefer for loop because we are iterating over a sequence.

Syntax of a for loop,

```
for item in sequence:
        #statements
```

In above syntax,

item is a variable that holds iterables from the sequence for each iteration.
Loop continues until we reach the last item in the sequence.

Note:

If you want to find a sequence of a number in that case you can use range() function in python.

range() function returns a sequence of numbers, starting from zero by default, and increments by 1(by default), and ends at a specified number.

Syntax of a range() function is,

```
range(start, stop, step)
```

Where start is a starting number which is zero by default if not mentioned. This is an Optional Parameter.

stop is an integer at which our iteration stops. This is a Required Parameter.

step parameter is an increment parameter that increments the value of the start parameter until it reaches the stop parameter. This is an Optional Parameter.

Flowchart of a for loop states that the body of for loop keep executing until the last item is reached.

For Example:

In this example we will print all the even numbers from zero to 99.

```
for I in range(100):
    if I%2==0:
        print(I)
```

Output all the even numbers from zero to 99.

List Comprehension

List comprehension is useful when we are appending values in a list using for loop.

With the help of list comprehension we can perform same appending operation in a single line.

Syntax of List Comprehension

my_list = [expression for item in iterable if condition == True]

Above syntax states that for an item if a condition returns True then that item will be appended to my_list.

Difference between for loop and list comprehension:

Let's differentiate these two terms using a simple program.

Problem Statement : Append from 0 to 5.

Case 1: Using for loop

```
my_list=[]
for I in range(5):
        my_list.append(I)
```

Case 2: Using List Comprehension

```
my_list=[I for I in range(5)]
```

Output Of Case 1 And Case 2 is same: [0, 1, 2, 3, 4]

As you can see the approach we used in a for loop is little time consuming if we have a large piece of code whereas using list comprehension, we can perform same task in a single line of code.

while loop

while loop is use for executing same block of code until the condition returns False.

while loop is differ from for loop because for loop works on iteration of a sequence whereas while loop works on a set of statements until condition returns False.

For Example:

Suppose that our task is to print fibonacci series from 0 to 34. In this case, we prefer while loop because we repeat same set of statements until we reach 34.

Syntax of a while loop:

```
while condition:
    #statements
```

Above syntax states that the while loop executes same set of statements until the condition return False.

Flowchart of a while loop states that before entering in while loop first interpreter checks condition followed by while loop(multiple times), if true then executes body of while loop otherwise exit.

For Example:

In this example we will print all the numbers less than 5.

```
number=0
while number!=5:
    print("number")
    number+=1
```

O/p- 0
1
2
3
4

Nested Loop

Nested loops are sequence or chain of loops inside another loop.

Syntax Of Nested for loop:

```
for item in sequence:
        for item_2 in sequence:
                statements(s)
        statements(s)
```

Syntax Of Nested while loop:

```
while expression:
        while expression:
                statement(s)
        statement(s)
```

Loop(for or while) inside another loop(for or while) is called Nested Loop.

Note:

In Python, we can also use else statement with loops.

else statement in python executes if and only if the loop is not terminated by break statement.

In next topic we will discuss about break and continue statement

For Example :

Let's check all the prime number in an interval.

```
lower=1
upper=10
for num in range(lower, upper+1):
        for i in range(2, num):
```

```
        if num%i==0:
            break
    else:
        print(num)
```

O/p- 1
    3
    5
    7

break and continue

In Python, break and continue statement alters the normal flow of loop.

Where break statement is used for terminating loop in between and continue statement is used for skipping the rest part of a loop and returns the control to the beginning of the loop.

Syntax for using break statement

```
        for item in sequence:
            if condition:
                #statement
            else:
                break
```

Syntax for using continue statement

```
        for item in sequence:
            if condition:
                continue
            else:
                #statement
```

Chapter 5: Functions And Modules

In our everyday life we use a word "reusable" and this word "reusable" plays a crucial role in programming.

In programming suppose that we have a set of elements and we have to perform same operations on few elements of that set. So do we need to write same code for same operation for different elements? To overcome from this problem, programming languages introduced Functions.

Functions

A function is a block of code that contains multiple statements and executes when it is called.

We can pass data as a parameter to the function and also function can returns data as an output.

Syntax To Write A Function

```
def function_name(para_1, para_2):
    #statement
    #statement
function_name()
```

Note:

- In python, we can define a function using def keyword.
- para_1 and para_2 are the parameters that we pass during function call(we can pass any number of parameters).
- To call our function, we use function name followed by parenthesis.

For Example :

Let's write a program to add two numbers using functions.

```
x=2
y=4
def func(a, b):
        return a+b

t=func(x, y)
print(t)
```

Above function func(a, b) taking x and y as a and b respectively and returning sum of a and b where the variable t will hold the result returned by func(a, b) and prints sum of x and y.

*args and **kwargs

Suppose that we have large set of sequence to pass as a parameter or we are unaware of the number of parameters we want to pass.

In above cases we use *args and **kwargs.

*args : We use *args when we are unaware of the number of parameters to pass.

For Example:
```
def func(*args):
        print("Hello "+ args[2])
x=["Rahul", "Ryan" , "Raj"]
func(x)
```
O/p- "Hello Raj"

*args take parameters as a tuple and, we can give any name in place of args to our parameter but * is necessary before the parameter name.

**kwargs : Functionality of **kwargs is similar to functionality of *args but the difference is, In **kwargs we pass parameters in the form of key=value and **kwargs accepts the passed parameters as dictionary.

For Example:
```
def func(**kwargs):
        print("Hello "+ kwargs['fname']
func("fname"= "ABC", "lname"="XYZ")
```
O/p- "Hello ABC"

Lambda Function

Lambda function is also known as Anonymous function because lambda function defined without a name.

We define lambda function for short duration or for small set of input.

Lambda function is defined using lambda keyword whereas normal function is defined using def keyword.

Syntax of Lambda Function:

lambda parameters : expression

In lambda function we can pass any number of parameters.

Lambda function can hold multiple parameters but for a single expression.

Lambda function returns the executed result so we can store the executed result in a variable and use it later.

For Example:

```
x=lambda a, b: a*b
print(x(2,3))
```
O/p- 6

map() function

In Python, map() function passes each item of an iterable to the function without a function call.

Syntax Of A map() function:

```
map(function_name, iterable)
```

For Example:

```
def myfunc(num):
    return num*2

my_nums=[1,2,3,4]

for item in map(myfunc, my_nums):
    print(item)
```
O/p- 1
    4
    6
    8

In above example we defined a function myfunc and an iterable my_nums which we passed in our map function respectively.

filter() function

The filter() function constructs an iterator from elements of an iterable for which a function returns true.

Syntax Of filter() function:

```
filter(function_name, iterable)
```

For Example:

```
def myfunc(num):
    return num%2==0
my_nums=[1,2,3,4,5,6]
print(list(filter(myfunc, my_nums)))
```

O/p - [2, 4, 6]

Variables Scope

Local Variable: The variables created inside a function are called local variables and

Local variables can be used only inside that respective function in which they are created.

For Example:

```
def myfunc():
    x=500
    print(x)
```

```
            myfunc()
```

O/p- 500

Global Variable: The variables created globally are called global variables.

Global variables can be accessed globally and locally.

For Example:

```
        x=200
        def myfunc():
              print(x)
        myfunc()
```
O/p- 200

Note : We can modify value of a global variable inside a function using global keyword.

For Example:
```
        x=200
        def myfunc():
            global x
            x=400
            print(x)
        print(x)
        myfunc()
```
O/p- 200
    400

Before calling our function the value of x will be 200 but after function call using global keyword we changed the value of x to 400.

Modules

Modules are collection of functions that we can import in our code anytime.

To create a module in python we just need to save our python code with .py extension.

Syntax For Importing a module:

import module_name

Syntax For Importing a module with another name:

import module_name as new_name

We can give any name to our module using as keyword.

If you want to know all the function name and variable names of the module you imported then you can use dir() function.

So, this is how we make modules in python.

Chapter 6: Object Oriented Programming

Object Oriented Programming is a programming methodology that uses class and objects to implement real world scenarios.

Python is an object oriented language, everything in python is object. The data structures we use in python are objects(list, tuples etc).

But still python is not 100% object oriented because python doesn't support strong encapsulation.

Objects

According to Object oriented programming, everything is an object which consists of some state and behavior.

For Example : According To Object Oriented Programming a car is also an object where car name denotes its state and car is used to ride, denotes its behavior.

Classes

Class is a concept that came from word classification which means objects with similar types of state and behavior are grouped together in to a same category called classes.

Syntax to write a class and an object:

```
class class_name:
        #class_variables
        #class_methods

    obj_name=class_name(parameters)
```

To create a class in python we use class keyword and class_name.
Inside our class we define class methods(also known as class functions)and class variables.
To create an object in python we write object name.

Syntax to access class methods and variables using object are:

```
        obj_name.method_name()
        obj_name.variable_name
```

First Program On Class And Object:

```
        class Hello:
            def hey(self):
                print("Hello")
        my_obj=Hello()
        my_obj.hey()
```

O/p - Hello

You might wonder why I used self as my function parameter.
The self is used to represent the instance(object) of the class.
With this **keyword**, you can access the attributes and methods(of particular object) of the class in **python**.

Dunder or Magic Methods

Dunder methods are the special methods used in a class to perform specific functionalities. Dunder stands for Double Underscores because all the dunder methods are followed by double underscores in prefix and suffix.

Few dunder methods are :

1. __init__
2. __str__

Let's discuss all the dunder methods one by one:

__init__ : This method invoked when an object of a class is created. __init__ dunder method is very useful to initialize the class variables(attributes).

For Example:

```
class myclass:
    def __init__(self, data):
        self.data=data
my_obj=myclass(10)
print(my_obj.data)
```

O/p- 10

__init__ method initialize 10 to a class attribute and using that instance we printed value of that attribute.

__str__ : This method is used for generating string output for end user.

The print statement and str() built-in function uses __str__ to display the string representation of the object.

For Example:

```
class myclass:
        def __init__(self, data):
                self.data=data
        def __str__(self):
                return self.data
my_obj=myclass("Hello Ryan")
print(my_obj)
```

O/p- Hello Ryan

Inheritance

Inheritance is the process by which one object acquires state and behavior of another object.

The process of creating a new class which inherits states and behavior of existing class is known as Inheritance.

Existing class is known as base class and class which inherits base class is known as derived class.

For Example : A child inherits state and behavior of his or her mother.

Syntax To inherit a class:

```
class derived_class_name(base_class_name):
        #attributes or methods
        #attributes or methods
```

For Example:

```
class Father:
    def __init__(self):
        print("Father Here")

    def whoAmI(self):
        print("I Am Father")

    def age(self):
        print("I Am 32")

class Child(Father):
    def __init__(self):
        Father.__init__(self)
        print("Child Here")

    def whoAmI(self):
        print("Child")

child=Child()
child.whoAmI()
child.age()
```

O/p- Child Here
     Father Here
     Child
     I Am 32

In this example, we have two classes: Father and Child. The Father is the base class, the Child is the derived class.

The derived class inherits the functionality of the base class.
- It is shown by the age() method.

The derived class modifies existing behavior of the base class.
- shown by the whoAmI() method.

The child's __init__() function overrides the inheritance of the parent's __init__() function.

To keep the inheritance of the parent's __init__() function, add a call to the parent's __init__() function.

Chapter 7: Errors And Exceptions

During writing our code we make common mistakes like indentation mistakes, mistakes related to syntax etc, and all these mistakes are termed as errors.

For Example, syntax error during writing our code.

Whereas, sometimes we do logical mistakes too which raises errors during runtime and these logical mistakes are termed as exceptions.

For example, when we try to divide a number by zero or array is accessed outside of its index, or when required memory is not available etc.

Exceptional Handling

The error handling mechanism consists of two parts, one is to detect errors and throw exceptions, and other is to catch the exceptions and take the appropriate actions.

Exceptional handling is a technique to handle the occurrence of exceptions that prevents abnormal terminations.

In exceptional handling we use try, except, finally and else keywords to handle all types of exceptions.

try, except, finally & else

- **try:** try block is used for detecting errors in our code.

- **except:** except block is used for handling errors detected from try block.
- **finally:** finally block executes whether try block raises errors or not.
- **else:** else block executes only if no errors detected in try block.

Syntax of try, except, finally, else:

```
try:
    #statements
except:
    #statements
finally:
    #statements
else:
    #statements
```

You can add any number of except block in your code.

For Example:

```
def input_int():
    try:
        x=int(input("Enter An integer "))
    except:
        print("Sorry you forgot")
    finally:
        print("I always executes")
    print(x)
```

Some of the common builtin exceptions are:

Exceptions	Description
ImportError	Raised when import statement troubles loading a module.
NameError	Raised when variable is not defined.
IndexError	Raised when we retrieving wrong index.
KeyError	Raised when dictionary of key is not found.
OSError	Raised when system returns system - related issue.

For more builtin exceptions visit : https://docs.python.org/3/library/exceptions.html

We can also write except block for particular exception.

For example:

```
try:
        doc = open('myfile','r')
        doc.write('Hello World')
except IOError:
        print("Could not find file or read data")
else:
        print("Successfully Updated")
        doc.close()
```

O/p - Could not find file or read data

Here we done with basics of errors and exceptions.

Chapter 8: File Handling

In our everyday life we deals with files and the file systems. For example we create new files, we write new or existing files, we read existing files, we delete existing files etc and all these actions related to files are considered as file handling.

What Are Files ?

A file is collection of data or information which stores in our system. One can read and write data anytime by accessing these files from their systems.

Different modes of accessing a file:

- **r** : Opening our file for reading purpose.
- **w** : Opening our file for writing purpose.
- **a** : Opening our file to append data at last.
- **r+** : Reading and writing our file.
- **w+** : For writing and reading(Overwrites a file or create a new file).

Open a file,

If we have an existing file in our system and if we want to access that file in that case we use open() to open a file.

For Example:

myfile=open("myfile.txt")

If file is stored in current directory then we can retrieve it using its name only but if the file is stored somewhere else then we have to specify full path.

For Example:

                myfile=open("D:/python/myfile.txt")

Reading a file,

To read this file(myfile), we use read() method,

For Example:

                myfile.read()

With this method you can read your file easily but when you try to read this file again in that case this will show empty string because during reading our file the cursor reached at the end of the file.

For reading our file again,

                myfile.seek(0)
                myfile.read()

.seek() method with zero index will take cursor to starting index and you can read your file again.

But if you want to read your existing file in a list format then use: myfile.readlines().

Above statement will return your file in a list format.

To close your file,

                myfile.close()

If you done using with your file then above statement will help you to close that file.

In above .read() method we have to close our file manually but if you want to avoid closing files manually then you can read your file,

```
with open("myfile.txt",mode='r') as my_new_file:
        contents=my_new_file.read()
```

Above statements are little complex but if you want to avoid manually closing of your file then above statement works well.

Writing a file,

If you want to write a file in that case also two conditions exists,

1. You want to write a new file.
2. You want to write in an existing file.

Case 1:

When you want to write a new file, use "w" mode and .write() method to add your information.

For example,

```
with open("myfile.txt",mode='w') as my_new_file:
        My_new_file.write("Your Text")
```

Case 2:

When you want to write in an existing file, use "a" mode and .write() method to add your information.

For example,

```
with open("myfile.txt",mode='a') as my_new_file:
        My_new_file.write("Your Text")
```

Passing the argument 'a' opens the file and puts the pointer at the end, so anything written is appended.

Let's discuss all these steps(opening, writing, reading and closing) in a single program.

```
with open("myfile.txt",mode='r+') as my_new_file:
        content=my_new_file.read()
        print(content)
        my_new_file.write("Your Text")
        print(content)
```

So here we completed and took basic knowledge of file handling in python.

- Thank you to those who continued to encourage me throughout the entire publishing process.

- Thank you to those who purchased my book.

- Thank you to those who recommend it to their friends and continue to spread the word.

- Thank you to everyone who has reviewed my book.

- Thank you to everyone who has taken time out of their day to read it.

- Thank you to everyone who has sent me honest and kind words - it means more than you know.

At last, if you enjoyed learning from this book, then do us a favor, would you please drop a review for this book on Amazon? It'd be greatly appreciated!

Please Let Me Know If You Have Any Further Queries:

officialsaxenarahul0708@gmail.com

www.ingramcontent.com/pod-product-compliance
Lightning Source LLC
LaVergne TN
LVHW081804050326
832903LV00027B/2084